Beyond our
Fears

Following Jesus in Times of Crisis

Pam Driedger

Faith & Life Resources

A division of Mennonite Publishing Network
Mennonite Church USA and
Mennonite Church Canada

Scottdale, Pennsylvania
Waterloo, Ontario

Beyond our Fears
Following Jesus in Times of Crisis
By Pam Driedger

Copyright © 2009 by Faith & Life Resources, a division of Mennonite Publishing Network, Scottdale, PA 15683 and Waterloo, ON N2L 6H7

Faith & Life Resources gratefully acknowledges the financial support of Mennonite Disaster Service for this project. Thanks also to steering committee of Gordon Friesen and Lois Nickel of MDS, Janet Plenert of Mennonite Church Canada, editor Byron Rempel-Burkholder of Faith & Life Resources, and the consulting group from across North America who offered ideas and support for the project.

Unless otherwise noted, Scripture text is quoted, with permission, from the New Revised Standard Version, © 1989, Division of Christian Education of the National Council of Churches of Christ in the United States of America.

International Standard Book Number: 978-0-8361-9476-0
Cover and book design by Merrill R. Miller
Cover Photo: iStockphoto/Helene Canada
Printed in USA

Orders and information:
USA: 800-245-7894
Canada: 800-631-6535
www.mpn.net

Contents

*Keep watch because you do not know the day or the hour.
—Matthew 25:13*

Faith is not just about trusting God to provide light when we find ourselves in the darkness of a crisis. Faith also means preparing, before the crisis comes, to carry God's light.

Story: Carmen almost loses her faith when Hurricane Katrina destroys her house in Pass Christian, Mississippi. When volunteers from Mennonite Disaster Service come to rebuild her house, she trusts God again and devotes her time to helping others in need.

Bible text: Matthew 25:1-13—The parable of the bridesmaids.

Neither this man nor his parents sinned; he was born blind so that God's works might be revealed in him.—John 9:3

It is natural for us to ask who or what is responsible for a crisis. The Scriptures, however, call us to focus on the opportunities we have to show God's grace and compassion, regardless of who is at fault.

Story: Nothando and her friend Abeni find their lives turned upside down by the AIDS epidemic in Zimbabwe, southern Africa. Despite the prejudices and fears of their family and friends, they choose to care for those who are suffering, regardless of their background.

Bible text: John 9:1-34—The man born blind.

3. Service Overcomes Self-Preservation 21

Let each of you look not to your own interests, but to the interests of others. Let the same mind be in you that was in Christ Jesus ...
—Philippians 2:4-7

Our human reaction is to escape or to build walls of protection around ourselves when our health or safety is threatened. God calls us to be prudent, but also to follow Jesus, who gave his own life in service to others.

Story: A strange disease, SARS, threatens to spread throughout Toronto in the spring of 2003. Amanda, a nurse, must wear protective clothing at work, and is quarantined at home. But she knows that she is doing what God has called her to do: care for sick people, no matter what the personal risks.

Bible text: Philippians 2:1-11—God comes as a human servant.

4. Living in Hope Overcomes Darkness 27

If you ... satisfy the needs of the afflicted, then your light shall rise in the darkness and your gloom be like the noonday.—Isaiah 58:10

The light of God will shine in the darkness of any crisis as the church participates faithfully and courageously in God's restoring work.

Story: In 1666, two local church leaders convince the people of Eyam, England, to voluntarily quarantine their village to keep the bubonic plague from spreading to neighboring communities. Today the village is still remembered as a beacon of sacrificial love.

Bible text: Isaiah 58:1-12—A promise of light.

Appendixes 33

1. **Bishop Cyprian Leads a Caring Movement**
   A story based on the witness of the church during the plagues of the third century.

2. **Resources for Further Reading**

Author 40

Introduction

What would happen in your neighborhood or your church if an unusual number of people were hospitalized? What if a pandemic, a natural disaster, or an act of terrorism hit your community? Would you seek safety, or would you take risks in order to help others?

Most of us would rather not think about scenarios like that, at least not right now. But governments and municipalities are creating plans to be prepared for each of these crises. Shouldn't we, as ordinary people of faith, be spiritually prepared? Why not know before the crisis what kinds of actions and attitudes are most consistent with our faith? How is God calling us to be good stewards of the future?

For several years, medical authorities have been warning that the world is due to suffer a flu virus on a global scale, equal to or greater than the international pandemic of 1918. They warn that, despite our advanced medical technology, thousands of people will die, and many more will become sick. People will fear for their health. Naturally, people will want to protect themselves.

How will the church respond to a flu pandemic? Do we have a plan? Will we retreat in fear, or are we ready to be God's light in the midst of suffering?

Crisis has always been a fact of human existence on this planet, and it can hit without warning. Unfortunately for us in North America, our technology and our wealth have led us to believe that we are safe; still, crises do come to our doorstep, as we have seen in Hurricane Katrina of 2005 and the SARS crisis of 2003.

In other countries, people are living with crises that are

hard for us to imagine. People in sub-Saharan Africa are coping with the huge AIDS pandemic—and with other health crises such as malaria and food shortages. The people of Southeast Asia are still coping with the unspeakable damage of the 2006 tsunami. People in Colombia, Iraq, and Palestine live in the midst of armed conflict.

This book has been written not to raise our fears but to do the exact opposite: to prepare the church to shine as God's light in the midst of such crises, to respond to our call to be people of healing and hope.

Even if these crises never occur this book will help us think through our mission as Christians. God calls us to join the work of healing and hope in our families, neighborhoods, and world, regardless of circumstances.

How to use this book

This book was designed to be part of a congregational study series, but it can also be a personal resource for inspiration and learning. Here are some suggestions for its use:

Group study. Each person should have a copy of the book for reading and reflection between sessions. The group leader should also have a leader's guide, which contains step-by-step suggestions for an active learning experience. That book also includes worship resources and suggestions for children's activities.

Individual use. Take time to ponder the reflection questions. Write your answers in a journal or notebook so you can go back and reflect on your thoughts.

Congregational pandemic preparedness. This study series is part of a larger set of resources that are being offered to the church as it learns about, and prepares for, the predicted flu pandemic in North America. For more information see page 38, or go to: www.churchpandemicresources.ca

***Beyond our Fears* guide for leaders**

Orders and information:

USA: 800-245-7894
Canada: 800-631-6535
www.mpn.net

1

Faith Overcomes Fear

Keep watch because you do not know the day or the hour.—Matthew 25:13

Faith is not just about trusting God to provide light when we find ourselves in the darkness of a crisis. Faith also means preparing, before the crisis comes, to carry God's light.

Bible text: Matthew 25:1-13—The parable of the bridesmaids.

We must make basic choices in the face of any crisis, large or small. Will our response be one of faith, or one of fear? Will we be prepared ahead of time, or will we avoid thinking about hypothetical situations and just see what happens? The following story is about Carmen, a woman from the Gulf Coast in Mississippi. Her life was disrupted by a crisis that is familiar to most of us, even if we did not experience it ourselves: Hurricane Katrina.

I Thought God Would Take Care of Us

For days, the news had been full of warnings about the hurricane. "This one might be as bad as Camille," the weather forecasters said. "It might be even worse …" Carmen wasn't too worried, though. Floods, hurricanes, and dire predictions were a part of life along the coast. On Sunday morning she and her children would go to Jackson to wait out the storm. They would leave as they had so many times before, and they would be back again in a few days. She wasn't looking forward to the cleanup. But she and her children would manage.

Saturday night, Carmen went out to walk along the beach. "That was my Godly place," she recalls. "Whatever was going on in my life, I could sit on the beach and look at the stars and find my peace. That night everything looked so pretty. The sea was calm and I could see lights from the houses and the stars shining in the sky. There was no sign of a storm coming. I remember thinking, *It's too beautiful for anything really bad to happen. The people here are such good people. We always take care of each other. I know God will take care of us.*"

When Carmen left town on Sunday morning, her faith was strong. She wasn't even worried about two of her brothers who had decided to stay and ride out the storm. After all, they would be in a house that hadn't even flooded during hurricane Camille!

The wind and the rain started early Monday morning. At 9:30 Carmen called her older brother. When he said that things were "pretty bad," she reassured him that it shouldn't be much longer; the storm was supposed to pass by 12:30. She couldn't miss the fear in his voice when he responded, "12:30. Oh, Good Lord. I don't know if we can last that long." Then the phone went dead. Carmen was left to imagine what was happening to her brothers as Hurricane Katrina raged throughout the day, preventing any further phone communication.

Tuesday morning Carmen headed home. She had to find out what had happened. She was forced to park about three miles from her brother's house because of impassable roads. She slipped and slid through foul smelling hurricane mud, passing one ruined home after another, and fearing what she would find when she reached her brother's house. At last she rounded a corner and saw that her brothers' house was still standing. Both brothers were out front, alive!

After the crying and hugging Carmen asked about the other houses. Mama's house? "Gone." The houses of each of her other brothers ? "Gone, gone, gone." Her house? Her brothers looked away. They said they hadn't been to her house. She would have to go see for herself.

"The whole town looked like someone put it in a bag full of mud, shook it up and tossed it back out. There was no order at all. There were cars, buses and houses thrown everywhere. When I got to my yard, it was empty. My beautiful old trees were gone, and my house was gone. I knew the house must be somewhere; so I climbed a fallen tree to look around. My house was in the middle of the next street on the wrong side of my neighbor's house.

"I walked over in shock. I tried to get my keys to work in the front door even though there was a huge hole in the wall and I could've just walked in. I got some clothes that we really needed. I wanted to find photos and my kid's trophies, but I couldn't see them and there wasn't room in the car. So I planned to come Saturday with a truck."

By Saturday, however, the town was locked down and Carmen wasn't allowed in. She was told not to worry; as soon as the streets were cleared, she would be able to go to her house and get her things.

The day the lockdown lifted, Carmen headed back. Finally she could rescue her precious mementos. Nothing had prepared her for what she found; her home was reduced to two piles of rubble, one on each side of the street, left by the bulldozer that had gone down the middle.

Carmen spent three weekends digging through the rubble trying to find the pieces of her life. "It was that third week when I found my son's baby shoe that something inside me broke. I sat down in the middle of the road and started screaming. 'God! How could you let something like this happen to us? This town was full of such good people! In 1995 when we lost everything in a fire, the people in this town helped us. Everybody always took care of each other. But now no one can help. Everybody's lost everything. What did we do to deserve this?'"

Hurricane Katrina

1. Hurricane Katrina was the sixth strongest hurricane to ever hit the U.S.

2. More than a million Gulf Coast residents were displaced from their homes. The number of deaths attributed directly or indirectly to the Hurricane was 1,836.

3. An estimated 80% of New Orleans was under water, up to 20 feet deep in places.

4. Hurricane Katrina caused $75 billion in estimated physical damages, the most costly hurricane in history.

Sources: National Geographic, National Oceanic & Atmospheric Administration (NOAA) Fox News, CNN, Discovery Channel

Reflect:

- How would you describe Carmen's faith just before the hurricane struck?

- Would your own reactions have been the same or different?

- Where is God in this story?

Part II

Carmen doesn't remember how long she sat in the street and cried, but eventually she concluded that she had two choices: to dig until she found her son's other shoe, or to get in the car, leave, and never return. She chose the car.

For over a month, Carmen refused to go back. She sent her 16-year-old daughter to live with an Aunt in Georgia, while she, her mother and her 10-year-old son stayed in Jackson, just waiting. "Every night my son would ask me if I had said my prayers. I would say to him, 'You pray for me, baby.' I was not going to pray ever again."

"Eventually my mama got a FEMA* trailer and I got a FEMA trailer and we went back. I started a job with the Boys and Girls Club. But I couldn't get any help to rebuild my life. No one would give me a loan because I didn't have anything and I hadn't been at my job for long enough. Of course not! I just came back. All I had was $2,000 from FEMA and $5,500 from insurance. When I couldn't get any help, it took me down even further. God was the furthest thing from my mind. I thought I would have to live in a FEMA trailer with nothing for the rest of my life."

One night in April, when her son was away, Carmen sat down at the computer her employer had given her. "I just sat in my trailer and I cried and I wrote. I wrote everything that had happened; I sent that letter to everybody and anybody who might help. I must have sent it to about 100 organizations and TV shows, some of which I had never even heard of before."

---

*Federal Emergency Management Agency, the U.S. government agency that dispenses disaster recovery aid.

A short time after she sent the letters Carmen came home to find a note on her door asking her to call someone from Samaritan's Purse. They had received her letter and they wanted to help. "When I called I asked what they could do for me. Would they loan me some money so I could start again? [The administrator] told me that they wanted to help me rebuild my house."

Samaritan's Purse wasn't building houses in Mississippi, but they were identifying needs and finding resources. "One day they came to visit and they told me that they had good news for me. The Mennonites were going to build me a house. I didn't know who the Mennonites were. I asked how they were going to build a house when I only had $5,500 dollars. They told me I didn't need to give anything."

Week after week, different people came to work on Carmen's house. She was amazed that they did not want anything from her. Sometimes they would ask her if she wanted to pray, but when she said "no" they accepted it. "I was grateful for all they were doing, but I was also bitter. I thought that these people could do this because they had everything in their lives. They didn't have any worries. Then I started talking to them, and I realized that they were just ordinary people with ordinary lives and they just wanted to help."

Carmen recalls one particularly wet and miserable day, the kind of day when no one wants to be outside. When she came home from work, she was surprised to find people working on her house. "I didn't want to be outside, but there was this group of almost strangers soaking wet and laughing while they got the concrete blocks ready for my house. I went out to them and I started to cry. That's when I got my faith back."

"It wasn't the house, although I'm thankful for the house. It was all the love that went into the house. The government failed us. The financial institutions failed us. But all of those ordinary people from all different places came to help. I came to love those people. They were my bits and

The volunteers who showed up to build Carmen's house were with Mennonite Disaster Service. MDS is a volunteer network through which people from Anabaptist churches can respond to those affected by disasters in Canada and the United States. In 2008, more than 4,800 people from across North America volunteered 26,316 days of labor to respond to disasters, rebuild homes, and restore lives. Projects were continued in the hurricane areas along the U.S. Gulf Coast and also in response to tornadoes (Kansas), floods (Iowa, Manitoba, British Columbia), and fires (California). For information on MDS, go to: www.mds.mennonite.net

pieces to put my life together and make me know that there is a God and whatever happens, he's going to fix it."

"I used to sneak into the house at night when the workers were gone. There are people's initials and little Scripture passages in all the walls. They're covered up so that you can't see them now. But I saw them, and I know that I am surrounded by love.

"Now I speak at lots of different events, not to get help for me, but to get help for other people. I have my blessings. But I have never felt the need to help others so much as I do now. Lot's of things will happen in life. When they do, we just have to press on and take care of one another."

Reflect:

- What triggered Carmen's return to faith?

- What were the results in her life?

- How might this story inspire you as you think about potential crises in your life?

Scripture Reflection

The parable of the wise and foolish bridesmaids.

Read: Matthew 25:1-13

This parable reflects a wedding custom that is very different from our own. It was quite familiar, however, to the people Jesus taught and it is still practiced in some cultures today. A group of young women are part of a nighttime procession that accompanies the bridegroom from the place of celebration to the couple's home. The "foolish" bridesmaids in the story assumed that the bridegroom would arrive at the expected time. They did not anticipate any delay, and they failed to bring extra lamp oil in case he was late.

But wouldn't it be easy to imagine a different ending to the story? Imagine that the bridegroom *does* arrive on time, and those who have brought exactly enough oil are praised for their strong faith in the bridegroom's punctuality, while those who purchased extra oil are criticized for wasting money because of their lack of trust?

Isn't the last ending more consistent with many sermons we hear, and with devotional writings we read? Trust God, they say. To the bridesmaids, they might say, "Don't stockpile oil, because that shows a lack of faith."

Sometimes it is difficult to distinguish between faith and foolishness. What is it that makes the bridesmaids with extra oil wise? In some of Jesus' other parables, planning doesn't always seem to be the wise choice. The man who plans to build bigger barns so that he can relax and enjoy the future is a fool (Luke 12:18-20). And why are the bridesmaids who ran out of oil criticized, while the woman who places all her savings in the temple treasury (Luke 21:1-4) is praised?

Should people of faith prepare for potential problems in the future, or should they trust that God will protect them? Carmen showed great trust the evening before she evacuated to Jackson. She felt God would take care of her. But when she found her house destroyed, she almost lost her faith.

What is faith and what is folly? What is wisdom and what is worry? These are not easy questions. But they do encourage us to examine our understanding of faith. We often think of faith as a bold action that may seem humanly impossible, but the Bible depicts faith as more of an attitude than an action. The single moments of complete trust are not the most important. Rather, it is our habitual attitude of faithfulness, a desire and an effort to maintain a relationship with God in good times and in bad that is most valued.

The wise bridesmaids were prepared to serve regardless of the circumstances that might arise, while the foolish bridesmaids were only prepared to serve if things went as expected. The man who wanted to build bigger barns was foolish because he never considered that God's plans might differ from his own. The poor widow was praised because her relationship with God was at the heart of her decision.

The parable of the wise and foolish bridesmaids ends with these words: "Keep awake therefore, for you know neither the day nor the hour." As people of faith we are called to be prepared to carry the light of God into the world at all times and under all circumstances. We hope and pray that calamity will not strike us. We believe that there will be times when God will answer our prayers and disaster will pass us by.

If we are honest with ourselves, however, we will admit that there have been many times when God has not answered the fervent prayers of faithful people in the way they might wish. They are not protected from harm. As we remember those times, we must also come to terms with the possibility that the darkness we dread may fall long before the world is put right again.

Preparing for the possibility that God may not give us what we have asked for doesn't mean we don't have faith. In fact, preparing our minds and hearts for such disappointments may be an act of profound faithfulness. The commitment to love God and others, for better or for worse, whether or not our prayers are answered, may take even more faith. Can we pray with our whole hearts for protection and, at the same time, prepare to serve God even if we are not protected?

When we pray for one thing and prepare to serve even if the opposite happens, we are saying that even though God's ways may not be our ways (Isaiah 55:8) and God's timing may not be our timing (Matthew 25:13), we still want to work with God.

Reflect:

- What crises have you experienced in your life? How did you cope with them?

- In a way, the "foolish" bridesmaids had faith: faith that the bridegroom would come on time. They felt they didn't need to prepare, because they "knew" how the future would turn out. What is wrong with this kind of "faith"?

- At what point does "preparing" go too far and become "worrying"?

- What can you, your family, and your church do to be better prepared for pandemics, natural disasters, or other crises?

2

Compassion Overcomes Blame

> *Neither this man nor his parents sinned; he was born blind so that God's works might be revealed in him.*—John 9:3
>
> It is natural for us to ask who or what is responsible for a crisis. The Scriptures, however, call us to focus on the opportunities we have to show God's grace and compassion, regardless of who is at fault.
>
> **Bible text:** John 9:1-34—The man born blind.

We all know about the AIDS epidemic that has swept through the continent of Africa, devastating families and communities. Some people ask how God can allow this. Others focus on the human failings that contribute to the problem. Some look upon AIDS as a call to love and care for others. Nothando and Abeni,* two women from Zimbabwe, are among the people who respond out of love.

Choosing to Love

When Nothando's husband fell ill, she had to stay home to care for him and their six children. The family needed food and money to pay for the mortgage and utilities—but there was no one who could go out and work. Before long, the electricity and water were cut off. The bank repossessed their home and put it up for sale. Since there was already an eco-

*Both Nothando and Abeni are assumed names.

nomic meltdown in Zimbabwe, life became desperate.

Nothando took her dying husband to the lawyers to show them how sick he was and how desperately the family needed help. The lawyer stopped them at the door and told them to leave. Unless they came with money, they were not allowed in the office.

Nothando and her family scraped by on the charity of family and fellow church members. Then, Nothando's husband died, and Nothando herself became sick and required surgery to correct a circulatory problem. She credits God with helping her to recover quickly from the surgery, but said that her mind and body remained tired. As she reflected on her own suffering, Nothando began to speak with God about all the difficulties experienced by women in Zimbabwe when their husbands, who are usually the breadwinners in the family, become sick or die. Then she began to think about the problems faced by women who get sick themselves and have no one to care for them.

Nothando realized that God was leading her to a ministry of caring for victims of HIV/AIDS. She received training as a home-based caregiver and now she takes care of nine people, two with cancer and seven with AIDS. The other members of her family are not completely happy about the work that Nothando is doing. She shares her scarce resources with other people, which leaves less for them.

There are also times when Nothando's family is afraid for her safety, because she works without much protection. When

AIDS by the numbers

The following statistics are from the UNAIDS 2008 Report on the global AIDS epidemic. The figures are for the year 2007.

33.0 million	people living with HIV/AIDS, including 15 million women and 2 million children; 22 million of the total are in Africa; 2 million are in North America and Europe
2.7 million	people newly infected with HIV in 2007
2.0 million	AIDS deaths
11.6 million	AIDS orphans in Africa
25 million	people who have died of AIDS since 1981
9.7 million	people in developing countries in immediate need of life-saving AIDS drugs; 2.99 million (31%) who are receiving the drugs

latex gloves are not available, she uses empty plastic sugar bags to hold or clean a patient. The bags are rough and sometimes the patients complain of pain. Sometimes they accuse Nothando of no longer caring about them.

Something else bothers Nothando. Ever since Zimbabweans have acknowledged the reality of the HIV/AIDS pandemic, many people have said that those who have AIDS should be left to suffer the consequences which they brought upon themselves through immoral choices. Nothando responds, "Who are you to judge people whom God created in his image?" When she talks to people who are angry about the unfaithful sexual behavior that has resulted in illness, she reminds them that God calls us to love and forgive.

This same call to love and forgiveness shapes the life of Nothando's friend Abeni. Not long ago, Abeni visited a church worker and asked him to pray for her. She said that her estranged husband was gravely ill with AIDS. He had been living with his parents, but when they heard of his "disgraceful plight" they wanted nothing further to do with him.

Abeni said that she had once made a sacred marriage vow to be faithful to this man, a promise that was now being put to the test. She decided that she would close her small shop and go to his village to care for him. But, she told the church worker, she expected the villagers to point at her and gossip about her, rather than offer help or sympathy. She needed prayer so that she could find the strength to "do what is required of me."

The church worker wondered if Abeni had told him the whole story; her husband had not only betrayed her, but may have also infected her with the virus that was destroying him. Despite what he had done, she was willing to give up her shop and her income for the love of God, and to be faithful to her vows. All she asked for was a prayer of support.

Reflect:

- Do you think Nothando and Abeni made the right choices?

- Are some people more deserving of care than others?

- If you were in Nothando's or Abeni's shoes, to what extent would your response be influenced by the counsel of others?

Scripture Reflection

The man born blind.

Read: John 9:1-34

Most of us are frightened by the possibility that we might experience pain and suffering. We learn how to identify sources of risk and avoid them whenever possible. When suffering happens to others, we find a certain amount of comfort in being able to find someone to blame. If we can find the cause of the calamity, we can look for ways to avoid similar suffering in our own lives. But there is a darker side to the blame game; if we blame someone else for the suffering, we feel less obligated to respond to the problem.

When Jesus' disciples see the blind man, they want to know two things: how much responsibility does he bear for his condition and, based on that, what is their obligation to help him? The disciples assume that God would not allow a completely innocent person to suffer. They believe that the man's blindness must be a form of punishment. Since the man has been blind all his life, they wonder if his blindness is a punishment for some sin that his parents committed, or if it is possible that he committed a sin even before he was born.

Jesus' response makes it clear that sometimes bad things just happen and no one is to blame. Jesus turns the disciples' attention away from laying blame, pointing out that they need to devote energy to making things better. "We must work the works of him who sent me [or, as some early manuscripts say, "of him who sent us"] while it is still day" (John 9:4).

In other words, we are called to do everything we can to make things better. Jesus invites his followers to see all suffering, regardless of its cause, as an invitation to act in God's name and to demonstrate God's unconditional love to the world. Jesus focuses on the response to suffering, rather than its cause. Jesus encourages us to see that God's will is not to be found in the suffering itself; rather, it is known in the love and care that we offer to those who are in pain.

Like many people today, the Pharisees of our story assume that suffering is part of God's will—part of the order established by God. They are horrified that Jesus is healing on the Sabbath. The Sabbath was to be a day of rest when all things are focused on God. According to the Pharisees, nothing that might appear to serve human purposes rather than God's plan is to be done on the Sabbath.

At the time of Jesus, certain acts, such as saving a person's life or even an animal's life (Matthew 12:11), were allowed on the Sabbath because they were understood to be acts that fit God's purpose. Other things were not allowed because they were seen as an effort to control life rather than trust God. In this story, the way the Pharisees question the man shows that they see Jesus' act of healing as an attempt to place human desires above trust in God's plan. They ask the man who was healed to acknowledge that his healing should not have taken place on the holy Sabbath. The Pharisees try to convince the man that Jesus is a sinner because of what he did.

It's also clear that the Pharisees assume the blindness would not have existed if God had not willed it. But the man refuses to get caught up in their argument about whether or not the blindness was a part of God's plan. He emphasizes that his healing could only have come from God and therefore must be part of God's plan.

Today, we don't typically accuse caregivers of interfering with God's plan when they care for sick or suffering people, regardless of the cause of the suffering. But we may give in to another temptation: *not* letting the example of these caregivers challenge us toward our own response of compassion and caring.

Like the Pharisees, we tend to make excuses for not helping people who are ill or suffering from a crisis. We may assume that the people are getting what they deserve. Some of us might even think that the suffering is part of God's plan.

This passage reminds us that we can never fully understand the reason for suffering. Instead, if we wish to participate in God's plan we must bring healing and hope to those who are the suffering.

Reflect:

- Think about specific diseases and natural disasters (AIDS, flu viruses, measles, tornadoes, hurricanes). To what extent is each of these caused by humans?

- When you meet or hear about people affected by these crises, how much do you blame them, the system, or God?

- How does your response to the last question affect the level of compassion you show toward those who are suffering?

3

Service Overcomes Self-Preservation

> Let each of you look not to your own interests, but to the interests of others. Let the same mind be in you that was in Christ Jesus...
> —Philippians 2:4-7
>
> Our human reaction is to escape or to build walls of protection around ourselves when our health or safety is threatened. God calls us to be prudent, but also to follow Jesus, who gave his own life in service to others.
>
> **Bible text:** Philippians 2:1-11—God comes as a human servant.

When the SARS crisis hit Toronto in the spring of 2003, the people of the city were full of fear. This wasn't an illness that killed only the very old and the very young; SARS was a highly contagious disease that also killed healthy people in their prime. SARS made people very sick very quickly and put anyone who was caring for them at risk. This story is about two health workers, Amanda and Joanna, who decided to live with the risks.

Choosing to Serve

Amanda was working as a nurse in a trauma unit in the heart of Toronto when the World Health Organization announced that SARS had made Toronto an unsafe city. Many of the patients in Amanda's unit were on artificial ventilation; nurses had to suction the patients' secretions regularly, greatly increasing the risk of contracting an airborne illness. Nevertheless, Amanda did not consider staying away from work.

Caring for people in need is not just what Amanda does—it's who she is. "I didn't dwell on the possibility of death because I came to terms with death a long time ago. You have to, to survive as a nurse. We see young people trip and hit their head and die, and old people fall in the same place and get up and walk away." Amanda couldn't imagine refusing to care for someone who was sick just because she might become ill. She had chosen long ago to live her life trusting God and accepting what came.

That trust and acceptance were put to the test when Amanda was sent into quarantine. She had to live behind a mask for ten days, only taking it off to sleep. A taxi picked her up each morning and took her home after work. She worked all day in a mask, gloves, and goggles. She ate alone and slept alone. She couldn't shower and she couldn't touch the other members of her family. She was restless and her family was scared.

Amanda responded to her family's fear with a combination of education and faith. She explained that her chances of getting sick were low. She named each risk factor and the precautions she had taken. She also reminded her family that risk is a part of life and the best way to respond to life's fragility is to treasure every moment and live it as fully as possible.

Not everyone joined Amanda in her renewed appreciation for the present. When Amanda went into quarantine, she received some less than friendly emails from people who had been at a school function with her a day or two earlier. The writers asked if Amanda had known that she was exposing them to this illness. Their fear of the future blocked out their compassion. But the anger of some was balanced by the support and concern of others who phoned or brought meals, or, in one case, even tried to visit her.

Like Amanda, Joanna believed that the two main factors

Severe Acute Respiratory Syndrome (SARS) is a respiratory disease caused by the SARS corona virus (SARS-CoV). Between November 2002 and July 2003, the disease threatened to become a pandemic, with 8,096 people worldwide reported to be infected, and 774 people dying (a case-fatality rate of 9.6%). In early 2003, SARS spread from the Guangdong province of China to 37 countries around the world. In Canada, the city of Toronto went on high alert due to a high number of reported cases. Conventions were cancelled and the tourism industry suffered acutely. Forty-three people in the city died of the virus.

that protected her from fear during the SARS crisis were knowledge and faith. Joanna's medical knowledge and expertise certainly helped her decide to care for others. She realized while talking about her experience that faith had also played a significant role in her decision.

Joanna remembers an encounter with another nurse who, like Amanda, had been placed in quarantine. As the other nurse walked toward her taxi, Joanna could see the exhaustion and stress on her face and in her eyes. Joanna went up to her and gave her a big hug. The other nurse burst into tears and said that Joanna was the first person who had touched her in a week.

What was it that enabled her to touch that nurse or visit Amanda at a time when other nurses wouldn't? Joanna remembers a moment of decision that happened in church.

"The minister said that we were going to pass the peace as we always did, but she knew that some people might be worried about SARS. She explained that if anyone chose not to shake hands, we would understand. I think people shook more hands that Sunday than they usually do. It was as if each one of us decided that there are some things that are more important than staying absolutely safe. I'm not saying that people should be foolish. Our minister talked to several health professionals before she decided to do what she did. It's just that human contact and love are as necessary for health as a lot of other things. I think that moment in church shaped the way I offered care."

Reflect:

- What strikes you the most about Amanda's and Joanna's responses to the SARS crisis?

- What roles did family and church play in their decisions?

- How would you have responded to the SARS crisis?

Scripture Reflection

God comes as a human servant.

Read: Philippians 2:1-11

The second half of our Scripture text was most likely a hymn that was used in the first century church. It summarizes the basics of Christian faith: God's coming to us in human form through Jesus, the crucifixion of Jesus, and the exaltation of Jesus through his resurrection and return to heaven. The writer, the Apostle Paul, uses the hymn to call the Philippians to lives of love and service to each other.

In his introduction to the hymn, Paul places particular emphasis on Christ's free choice. He calls his readers to "let the same mind be in you that was in Christ Jesus." In other words, make choices in the same way that Jesus did. Paul reminds us that although Jesus was divine and could have chosen to live with all of the power and prestige of God, he chose, instead, to live as a human and as a "slave."

Thankfully, slavery is not literally a part of our lives, though unfortunately it still secretly exists in some parts of the world. It hovers as a dark chapter of our North American history, and some of us have ancestors who were slaves. It may be hard, therefore, for us to catch the significance of Paul's words.

To understand this passage, we need to consider what it meant to be a slave in ancient times. A slave was someone whose identity was tied up with the identity of the person or family of the master. As an extension of the master, the slave could only care for himself or herself by caring for the master.

The early Christians said that Jesus took the form of a slave when he surrendered his right to self-preservation—when the well-being of others was his passion. As a "slave," Jesus found his purpose in caring for what belonged to the Master, God. Jesus received the honor that belongs to God—not by claiming his right to that honor, but by serving.

Jesus loved God and loved his neighbor as himself (Matthew 22:39). Paul suggests that we are also called to love and care for other people as we would ourselves. We are to empty ourselves of our individualism to see the well being of other people as a necessary part of our own well-being. As Paul says in 1 Corinthians 12:27, we are "one body in Christ." If we have in ourselves "the same mind that was in Christ Jesus," we cannot say "I need to take care of myself first." In Christ there is no "me" apart from "you."

This understanding of self stands in contrast to the view of today's society, which emphasizes the importance of individualism and independence. It is also quite different from the way people in the Roman Empire of Paul's day understood themselves. Caring for others was at the heart of the life of the early church. This became particularly evident during two devastating pandemics which swept the Roman Empire in 165 and in 251.* During both of these, Christians chose to care for one another and for their non-Christian neighbors even though it significantly increased their own chances of getting sick and dying. The behavior of the Christians was quite different from that of their pagan neighbors who avoided illness in the only way known at the time—by getting as far away as possible, leaving the sick to fend for themselves and the corpses of the dead to pile up.

There are several reasons that the Christians were willing to risk their lives to care for others, all of which can be found in this Scripture passage. First, they kept themselves in the mind of Christ. Loving and caring for one another had become the heart of who they were. To run away from someone who was in need would have been to run away from their beliefs. The only way to remain true to themselves was to stay and care for others.

The second reason was that Christians did not believe that death was the end; therefore, staying alive was not nearly as

"[The believers] held fast to each other and visited the sick fearlessly, and ministered to them continually, serving them in Christ. And they died with them most joyfully, taking the affliction of others, and drawing the sickness from their neighbors to themselves and willingly receiving their pains ... But with the heathen everything was quite otherwise. They deserted those who began to be sick, and fled from their dearest friends. And they cast them out into the streets when they were half dead, and left the dead like refuse, unburied. They shunned any participation or fellowship with death; which yet, with all their precautions, it was not easy for them to escape."

—from the "Festal Epistle" of Dionysius of Alexandria, ca. AD 260

---

*What follows is a brief summary of research detailed in: Rodney Stark, *The Rise of Christianity: a sociologist reconsiders history*, (Princeton, N.J.: Princeton University Press, 1996), pp. 73-94.

important as living well. For them, living well meant living as Jesus lived.

The third reason was that just as Jesus was "exalted" following his death and resurrection, the early Christians believed that God rewarded those who gave themselves in service to others.

Because Christians cared for one another during these epidemics, the percentage of deaths among Christians was not nearly as high as it was among the non-Christian population. When no other services were available, even elementary nursing care could greatly reduce the death toll. The higher survival rates among Christians, combined with the gratitude felt by non-Christians who owed their lives to Christian caregivers and in many cases became believers themselves, were significant factors in the rapid growth of the early Christian church. This event lends further weight to the promise implied in the Philippians passage: God will honor self-emptying love.

If we were faced with a similar situation, how would we react? How would we reflect "the mind of Christ"?

Reflect:

- Think about a time when you had to choose between your own safety and the safety of others. How did you decide whose safety was more important? What difference did the people's status make (whether they were friends or strangers, rich or poor)?

- How does our commitment to Christ affect our choices in these situations?

- The early church grew in numbers and in reputation when Christians put their own lives at risk for the sake of each other and their neighbors. Can you think of a contemporary parallel?

4

Living in Hope
Overcomes Darkness

> *If you ... satisfy the needs of the afflicted, then your light shall rise in the darkness and your gloom be like the noonday.—Isaiah 58:10*
>
> The light of God will shine in the darkness of any crisis as the church participates faithfully and courageously in God's restoring work.
>
> **Bible text:** Isaiah 58:6-12 — God's promise of restoration.

S cientists and medical experts tell us that it is not a question of if there will be another pandemic; it is only a question of when. Despite all our medical technology, they say there will be a time when one of the many viruses to which humans have no known immunity mutates in such a way that it could spread rapidly from person to person. When that happens, many people will get very sick, many will die, and all people of faith will be challenged to act faithfully in the face of fear.

It may be impossible to imagine exactly what a pandemic would mean for our community, but we can draw many lessons from history. In addition to the experience of the third-century church mentioned in Chapter 3 (see also the children's story about Bishop Cyprian, page 33), the journey of a village in England in the 17th century offers us an inspiring example of sacrificial love.

While we are unlikely to hear the cries of "bring out your dead" echoing through our communities in the way they did in the streets of Europe and England, we are likely to be *faced with some of the same questions they faced. Will we think first of our own safety or the needs of others? Will we try to run or will we stay to help? One way we can prepare to answer those questions is by imagining ourselves as members of a community which really asked them.*

A Village Quarantines Itself

It was the summer of 1665 in England. The bubonic plague was killing thousands upon thousands of people. All who were able were fleeing the cities; they hoped to escape death, but often carried death with them. The majority of the deaths had been confined to the southern part of the country while northern England had largely been spared.

Early in September, George Viccars, a tailor in the village of Eyam in Derbyshire, received a parcel of cloth from London. The cloth was damp, and when Viccars hung it out to dry, the plague-infected fleas that had been trapped inside were released. A week later, the tailor was dead. Soon others in the village began to sicken and die. When the winter arrived it seemed as if the plague had run its course, but with the warm weather of spring, it returned with a vengeance.

As illness and fear spread from house to house, the villagers began to pack up their things. They prepared to flee, hoping that they would be able to outrun death. Two church leaders in the village, William Mompesson and Thomas Stanley, challenged the villagers to rethink their decision to run. They reminded the villagers that if they fled to other parts of the country, they would carry the Black Death with them. Mompesson and Stanley quoted John 15:13 "No one has greater love than this, to lay down one's life for one's friends." They asked the villagers to put their Christian faith into action, accepting death themselves so that others might live.

The people of Eyam decided to accept a voluntary quarantine. All 350 members of the village agreed to do what they could to protect neighboring villages from the plague by allowing no one to come into or leave the village until the plague had run its course. When outsiders were seen coming down the road toward the village, sentries would call out, warning the outsiders of Eyam's infection with the plague. Merchants from neighboring towns would bring supplies to the outskirts of the village and collect the payment which the villagers left in containers filled with vinegar. Each family in Eyam agreed to bury their own dead quickly and close to their homes to minimize the spread of the disease. Church services continued, but they were held in the open air.

The Eyam quarantine lasted for five months and appears to have been honored by all of the villagers. When the plague had finally run its course, 260 people had died. At 75 percent of the population, that was a higher percentage than in any other community in England, but the quarantine accomplished its intended purpose. The plague did not spread to any of the neighboring communities. The village of Eyam earned its place in history. Over 300 years later, the sacrifice of many in this small community continues to inspire visitors from around the world.

Reflect:

- What do you think caused the villagers in Eyam to accept the voluntary quarantine?

- Could the same thing happen in your community today? Why or why not?

Scripture Reflection

A promise of light.

Read: Isaiah 58:6-12

Sometimes it seems as though God turns a deaf ear to our prayers. We do our part: we pray, we attend worship services, we are faithful, but still we suffer. Sometimes we experience some relief and we think things are finally

Established in love

In 1558, many in Amsterdam were dying from the plague. On November 14 of that year, Menno Simons, the leader of the persecuted Anabaptists, wrote the following to his flock:

Elect brethren and sisters in the Lord, I hear that the fire of pestilence is beginning to rage in your vicinity. . . . Be strong in the Lord, be of good cheer, be comforted. For your whole life and death is lodged in the hands of the Lord. All your hairs are numbered, and without Him not one shall drop from your head. The number of your days, nay, your life, is measured as by handbreadths by Him. Therefore do not fear but willingly serve each other in time of need. Oh, do not let the visiting of the sick vex you, for by this you shall be established in love . . . It is also the nature of true love to lay down our lives for [each other]. 1 John 3:16. . . .

—*From* The Complete Writings of Menno Simons, *edited by J. C. Wenger (Scottdale, Pa.: Herald Press, 1984), pages 1055-56* changing, but then the change stops and the problems return. It seems unfair. We look around and see that life is going well for other people and we ask why we have been forgotten.

This is the position in which the Israelites find themselves when God speaks to them through the words of Isaiah. The people have returned to their homeland, Judah, after years of exile in Babylon. They think their time of suffering is over. But life in Judah is hard; it seems as if God has abandoned the people once again. The people fast and pray, but they still face continual problems and hardships. Haven't they suffered enough? What does God want from them?

Our Scripture comes in the middle of Isaiah's response to this question. God wants the same thing from the people that God always wanted—their hearts. The reason that the prayers and fasts haven't changed the relationship between the people and God is that they are ritual words and actions that are disconnected from the everyday lives of the people.

Religious actions like prayer and fasting are important in the Bible, but they are not important because God needs them. They are important because they are tools for inner change; if they do not change us, they are useless.

When we offer our lives to God thinking that God should now do things our way, we show that our prayer is hollow. Similarly, fasting helps us focus on things that are important to God—reordering our priorities to align with God's purposes. God denounces the fasts of the Israelites because the people are hoping to change God rather than themselves.

Isaiah tells the people what really pleases God: "If you offer your food to the hungry and satisfy the needs of the afflicted, then your light shall rise in the darkness and your gloom be like noonday" (v. 10). This is not like a market transaction, as if food and comfort are what you must pay if you want God to give you joy. Rather, this is a simple observation: in the very act of caring for others, joy will come to you and life will not feel so dark and hopeless. The act of offering ourselves for others gives new meaning and purpose to our own lives. Isaiah goes on to say, "… you shall be called the repairer of the breach, the restorer of streets to live in" (v. 12).

Isaiah challenges the people to commit their lives to working for the thing they want to see. If they want everyone to have enough to eat, they should share what food they have. If they want injustice to end, they should assist those who are treated unjustly. If they want peace, they should stop pointing fingers and speaking ill of others.

This passage challenges us, too, to become part of the answer to our prayers. If we want God to free us from fear, we are invited to do what we can to help others find security. If we want God to bring us healing, we are invited to care for those who need healing. If we want to be sure that we will not be isolated during times of crisis, we are invited to keep people connected by nurturing good communication.

In many ways this may sound like the saying: "If you want something done well, do it yourself." The difference is that God's call to become sources of healing and hope is not an invitation to do it ourselves, but to be partners with God. The healing and the hope do not come because we are successful, but because we have joined God in God's restoring work. When we work with God, God's healing and hope become part of us. We can feel them even in the midst of the most difficult circumstances.

Reflect:

- How do you understand God's purposes in human history? Are they more concerned with this world or the next? With body, or soul?

- What is the relationship between prayer and action in responding to a crisis?

- As a result of your study and reflection in this book, what practical steps have you considered in preparing for potential crises in your community? What steps do you need to implement now?

Appendixes

1

Bishop Cyprian Leads a Caring Movement

By Rebecca Seiling

T*he following story is from the children's book,* Don't Be Afraid—Stories of Christians in Times of Trouble *(Faith & Life Resources, 2009). While the details are fictional, the story is based on the facts of Bishop Cyprian's courageous efforts to minister to the sick and dying of Carthage in the third century AD.*

Bishop Cyprian walked the streets of Carthage, praying under his breath, "God, relieve our suffering. Relieve our pain."

As he walked, Bishop Cyprian looked around, shaking his head sadly. Hundreds of people were dying each day, dying alone near the white stone buildings, uncared for because family and friends had deserted them. Dead bodies lay scattered on the cobblestone streets, with no one to claim them or give a proper burial.

Fifty-one-year-old Cyprian was a leader in the church in the North African city of Carthage, the third most important city in the Roman Empire. Born in the year AD 200, he had grown up the son of a wealthy senator. He had the best education possible. But all of this was in the past. At age 46, he became a Christian and gave up his wealth. Two years later, he was appointed as bishop—the leader of all the Christians of Carthage.

Every morning after breakfast, Cyprian walked along the streets of Carthage. Some days he passed by the shores of the Mediterranean Sea and saw the sparkling water as the warm sun shone down on it. Other days, he walked past the luxurious Roman bathhouses in the middle of the city.

Today, in the year 250, he walked by a dark, musty tavern where men sat talking, past the bakery where bread loaves browned in wood-fired brick ovens, past the fountain in the middle of the square where women filled their clay jugs of water for the day. Despite the activity of daily life, there was a heavy sadness that blanketed the city. A deadly plague had spread to Carthage.

Not one family had been spared from fear and grief. From the poorest slaves to the wealthiest Roman officials, everyone knew a friend or family member who was sick or who had already died. Carthage was now a city of suffering, sickness, death, and tears. It was a city in constant mourning.

Bishop Cyprian heard a desperate, low moan. Ahead of him, a man lay by the side of a building, coughing and groaning. His bony hands were clutching his chest, his weary eyes squinting at passers-by. He was a young man, possibly the father of young children. But this plague did not spare anyone, not even the young.

Cyprian walked quickly over to the man. "God's peace to you, young man," the bishop said as he bent down and put

his hand on the man's shoulder. With his other hand, Cyprian swatted flies from the young man's face.

"Help me," the man said quietly, barely able to speak through his parched, dry lips.

"God is with us in suffering," Cyprian said, "God will not leave you alone." The man opened his eyes a little and slowly lifted his head. His eyes were watery and empty, almost as if he was already dead.

"I have no one to help me. My family is gone, and my friends have left me for dead. How can you say I am not alone?" he asked, then began coughing violently.

The bishop looked the stranger directly in the eyes. "I will help you," Cyprian assured him.

"I am so afraid. What if I die?" asked the man.

"If you die, you will die with dignity, surrounded by people who care about you," the bishop responded. Cyprian took off his outer cloak, and covered the man's body with it. As he got up to leave, Cyprian promised to send help.

The man shook his head. "Why? Why are you doing this? You don't even know me!"

The kind bishop answered, "God knows you and loves you, my son. Rest now. I will get some of my friends, and we will come back for you soon. But please permit me to know your name."

"Donatus," the man said.

Bishop Cyprian walked briskly among the homes in his neighborhood, gathering the people of the church together. The picture of Donatus dying alone on the streets was clear in his mind, and it spurred him on as he knocked on the thick wooden doors of his neighbors. Many women, men, and children followed him to an opening in the street in a curious parade.

He cleared his throat and then spoke earnestly to the group, "My friends, people are dying alone on the streets of our city. It is our duty as followers of Christ to extend our hands to those in need, even if it means risking our own lives. We cannot abandon these people. They must be cared for and loved."

MANELLE OLIPHANT

A woman in the crowd was not so sure. "But some of these sick people are the people who have treated us badly because we're Christians. Why should we help them now?"

Bishop Cyprian nodded. "Yes, this is difficult," he said. "What I am asking you to do is not easy. But there is nothing wonderful about only loving our own people. Everyone does that. We must do better. We must extend forgiveness and overcome evil with good by loving those who have persecuted us. God makes the sun rise on us all. So let us do good to all."

Cyprian continued with his appeal. "We will help people no matter what their background may be. This is what God expects of us. Just this morning I met a young man who needs our help. Who can help to carry him to my home?"

Two young men volunteered to get Donatus. They found him huddled on the street, coughing, with Cyprian's cloak draped around him. They lifted Donatus so that his arms draped over their shoulders, and their own strong arms holding his back and his legs. In this way, they carried Donatus to Cyprian's home.

The two men lay Donatus down on a mat that Cyprian had prepared. Cyprian fed Donatus some warm broth, and then he sat near the lonely man as he drifted off to sleep. For Donatus, it was a great relief to have a comfortable place to rest, with someone beside him, caring for him and giving him shelter.

The other people of the church also began to bustle with acts of caring. Young men carried people from the streets to be cared for in homes. Families opened what little space they had in their homes to share it with strangers. An elderly woman made soup, and her granddaughter delivered it. A baker offered fresh loaves of bread. When people died, two women prepared their bodies for burial.

Many of the sick people they found on the streets had been completely abandoned by fearful family members who were afraid of catching the same illness. While others fled in fear, the Christians were inspired by Bishop Cyprian's compassionate words. They courageously sought out sick people and nursed them. Many people still died, but others came back to health. Those who had been sick quickly joined the church's mission to help others in need.

Weeks passed by. One evening, Bishop Cyprian sat at Donatus' bedside. Donatus had been coughing all day. His face was taut, his body thin. The bishop could see that despite his efforts, Donatus was not getting better. Through the open window they could both see the sliver of sun that was setting on the horizon

With a quiet, small voice, Donatus said, "Thank you, Bishop. God has healed my spirit and you've shown me God's love. I'm not afraid to die now."

Bishop Cyprian took the hand of this stranger whom he had befriended on the street. He said, "This is not the end, my friend. It is a new beginning in a place with no pain or crying."

Donatus smiled. He closed his eyes and took in one last, long breath. He breathed out, and then died peacefully.

As weeks and months turned into years, the plague raged on. For 15 long years, the deadly disease claimed the lives of hundreds in Carthage and thousands throughout the Roman Empire. Although it was a challenge to follow Jesus, the wise bishop knew it was the right way to live. This was a time to show courage and hope in God. Bishop Cyprian told the people, "God will reward you when you give yourselves in service to others."

Surprisingly, the church grew during this terrible time of sickness and death. Other people saw how caring the Christian community was, and they, too became Christians and joined the community. Former enemies became friends and many lives were saved. Hurtful wounds were healed; seeds of forgiveness were planted.

Because Christians cared for each other, many of them survived the deadly plague. Bishop Cyprian and the church in Carthage demonstrated that God's love can heal, and that God is always with us. These Christians showed that selfless love can triumph over hatred, sickness and even death.

2

Suggested Resources

Books

Roberts, Stephen B. and Willard W. C. Ashley, eds. *Disaster Spiritual Care: Practical Clergy Responses to Community, Regional and National Tragedy.* Woodstock, VT: Skylight Paths Publishing, 2008. The definitive guidebook for counseling not only the victims of disaster but also the clergy and caregivers who are called to service in the wake of a crisis.

O'Keefe, Betty and Ian Macdonald. *Dr. Fred and the Spanish Lady: Fighting the Killer Flu.* Surrey, BC: Heritage House, 2004. Tells of Dr. Fred Underhill and his battle against the 1918 Spanish influenza that killed 25 to 50 million people worldwide—a compelling story of people coming together in a crisis.

Long, Laurie Ecklund. *My Life in a Box: A Life Organizer.* Fresno, CA: AGL Publishing, 2008. Practical ways families can organize their important papers and possessions so they are ready when a major crisis comes.

Websites

Church Pandemic Resources
www.churchpandemicresources.ca

An online resource to help congregations prepare for and respond in the event of a pandemic. Sponsored by Mennonite Church Canada and Mennonite Disaster Service.

Eden Extension Disaster Network
www.eden.lsu.edu/LearningOps/FBO/

This link is for faith-based organizations dealing with pandemics and other disasters. The website has many other links to help communities and governments prepare for crisis.

Mennonite Church Canada Resource Centre
www.mennonitechurch.ca/resourcecentre/Home

Search by "disaster" or "pandemic" to find books and videos listed here and many others.

Mennonite Disaster Service
www.mds.mennonite.net/

The volunteer organization that offers a helping hand and a Christian witness in the wake of natural disasters and other crises.

CD

Faith Community Summit on Pandemic Preparedness and Response (Mennonite Church Canada; available through its resource center, above)

Coverage of the first-ever national forum of its kind in Canada, in 2007. Includes addresses by healthcare experts, government officials, and faith community leaders about the role faith groups will play during a major health emergency.

Author

Pam Driedger is the Director of Spiritual Care at Eden Mental Health Centre in Winkler, Manitoba, and a member of the Community Trauma Response Team for the Regional Health Authority of Central Manitoba. She has written and lectured extensively on the role of the church in health and healing. Pam attends the Altona Mennonite Church, where her husband Gordon serves as pastor.